Apatosaurus

Lori Dittmer

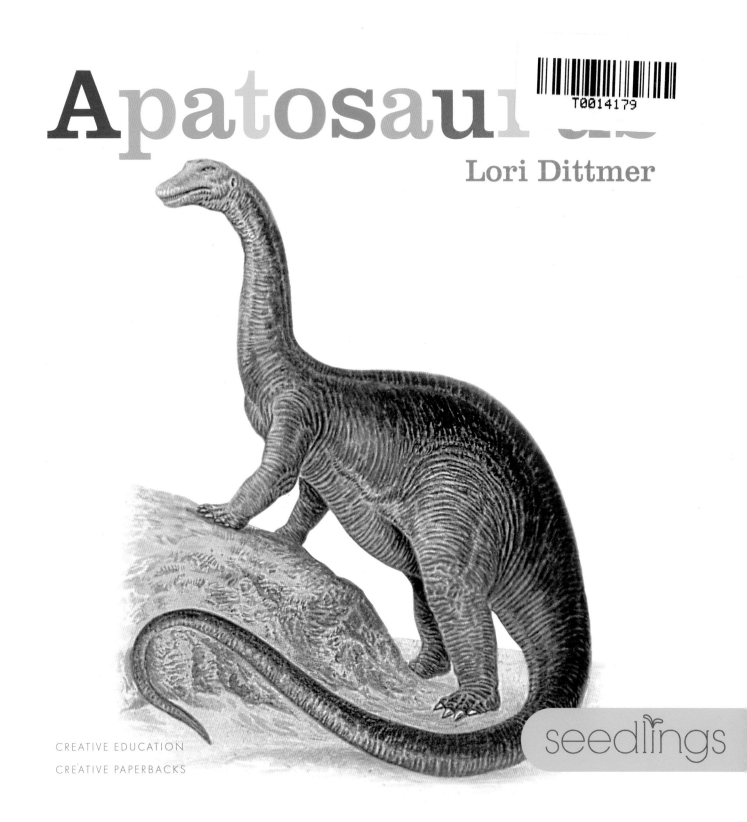

CREATIVE EDUCATION
CREATIVE PAPERBACKS

seedlings

Published by Creative Education and Creative Paperbacks
P.O. Box 227, Mankato, Minnesota 56002
Creative Education and Creative Paperbacks
are imprints of The Creative Company
www.thecreativecompany.us

Design by Ellen Huber
Production by Rachel Klimpel and Ciara Beitlich
Art direction by Rita Marshall

Photographs by Alamy (NAPA/Alamy Stock Photo, mark Turner), Corbis
(Louie Psihoyos), Getty (DEA Picture Library), Science Source (ROGER
HARRIS, Roger Harris/Science Photo Library, SEBASTIAN KAULITZKI,
STOCKTREK IMAGES), Shutterstock (Catmando, Elenarts, Daniel Eskridge,
Vac1), SVPOW (Matt Wedel), ThinkstockPhotos (danku), Wikimedia
Commons (Library of Congress Prints and Photographs Division)

Library of Congress Cataloging-in-Publication Data
Names: Dittmer, Lori, author.
Title: Apatosaurus / by Lori Dittmer.
Description: Mankato, Minnesota : Creative Education and Creative
    Paperbacks, [2024] | Series: Seedlings: dinosaurs | Includes bibliographical
    references and index. | Audience: Ages 4–7 | Audience: Grades K–1 |
    Summary: "Early readers are introduced to Apatosaurus, a Jurassic giant
    that was one of the largest land animals on Earth. Friendly text and
    dynamic photos share the dinosaur's looks, behaviors, and diet, based on
    scientific research"—Provided by publisher.
Identifiers: LCCN 2022013890 (print) | LCCN 2022013891 (ebook) | ISBN
    9781640265011 (library binding) | ISBN 9781682770535 (paperback) |
    ISBN 9781640006317 (ebook)
Subjects: LCSH: Apatosaurus—Juvenile literature. | Dinosaurs—Juvenile
    literature.
Classification: LCC QE862.S3 D583 2024 (print) | LCC QE862.S3 (ebook) |
    DDC 567.913/8—dc23/eng/20221104
LC record available at https://lccn.loc.gov/2022013890
LC ebook record available at https://lccn.loc.gov/2022013891

Printed in China

TABLE OF CONTENTS

Hello,
Apatosaurus!

This dinosaur lived long ago.

Diplodocus roamed at about the same time. *Stegosaurus* did, too.

O. C. Marsh found the first *Apatosaurus* fossils in 1877. He gave the dinosaur its name.

Apatosaurus weighed as much as five elephants. It stood on four thick legs.

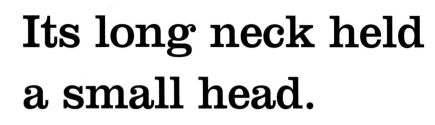

Its long neck held
a small head.

Apatosaurus might have cracked its tail like a whip! Or maybe its tail dragged on the ground.

This dinosaur pulled leaves from plants with its teeth. It swallowed without chewing.

Apatosaurus stretched its neck for food.

It spent most of
the day eating.

Goodbye, *Apatosaurus!*

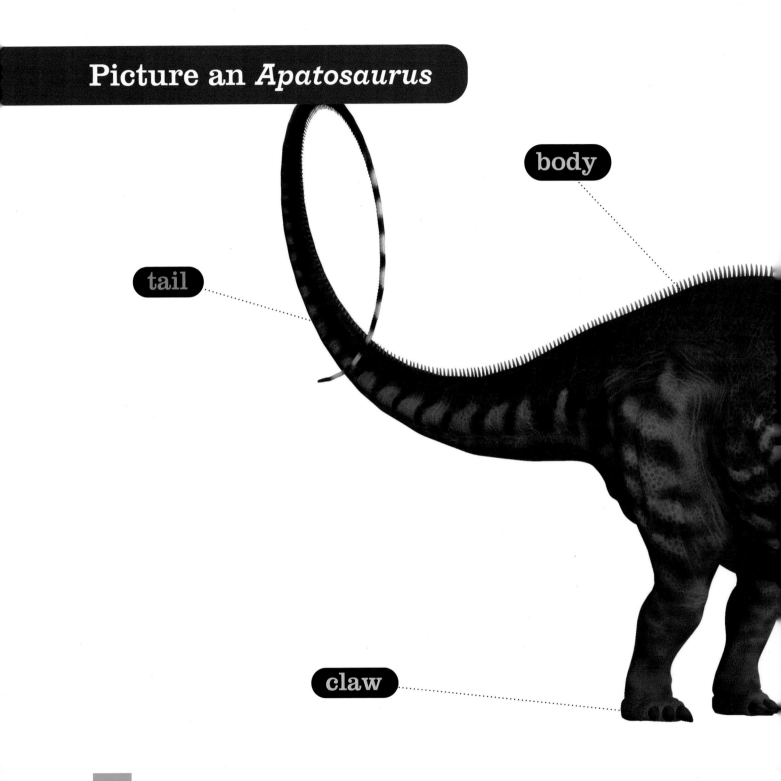

Picture an *Apatosaurus*

body

tail

claw

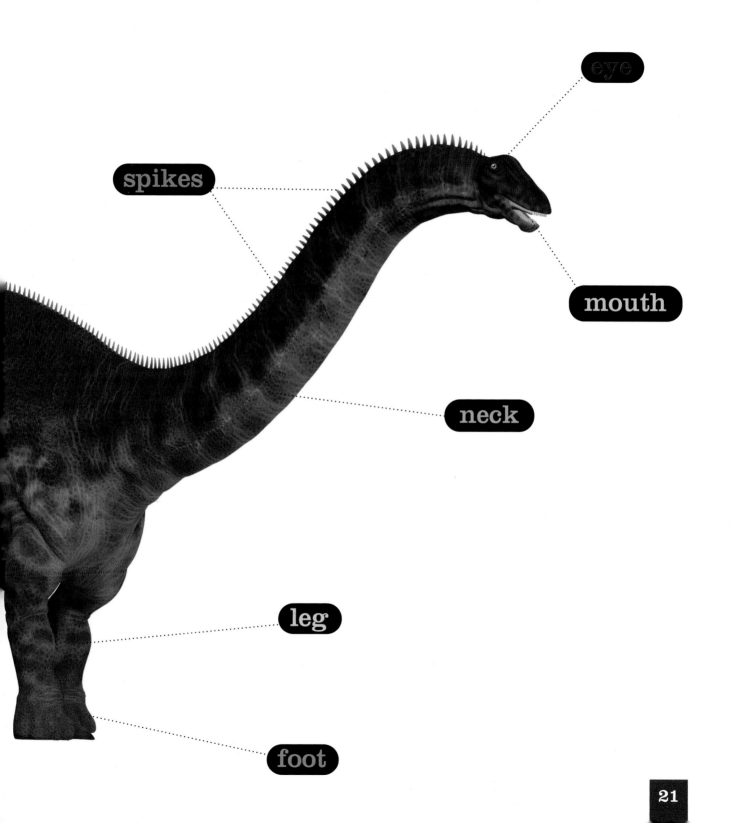

eye

spikes

mouth

neck

leg

foot

crack: to make a sharp, loud sound

fossil: a bone or trace from an animal long ago that can be found in some rocks

Read More

Gagne, Tammy. *Apatosaurus: A 4D Book*. North Mankato, Minn.: Pebble, 2019.

Storm, Marysa. *Apatosaurus*. Mankato, Minn.: Black Rabbit Books, 2021.

Websites

DK Find Out! | *Apatosaurus*
https://www.dkfindout.com/us/dinosaurs-and-prehistoric-life/dinosaurs/apatosaurus
Read more about *Apatosaurus* and take a dinosaur quiz.

Ducksters | *Apatosaurus* (*Brontosaurus*)
https://www.ducksters.com/animals/apatosaurus.php
Learn about the size of this dinosaur and where to see *Apatosaurus* fossils.

Note: Every effort has been made to ensure that the websites listed above are suitable for children, that they have educational value, and that they contain no inappropriate material. However, because of the nature of the Internet, it is impossible to guarantee that these sites will remain active indefinitely or that their contents will not be altered.

Index